THE EX PARADE

THE EX PARADE

A TONGUE-IN-CHEEK BUT TRUTHFUL DATING MEMOIR

By T.G. Pinheiro

iUniverse, Inc.
Bloomington

The Ex Parade
A Tongue-In-Cheek but Truthful Dating Memoir

iUniverse books may be ordered through booksellers or by contacting:

iUniverse
1663 Liberty Drive
Bloomington, IN 47403
www.iuniverse.com
1-800-Authors (1-800-288-4677)

ISBN: 978-1-4759-5767-9 (sc)
ISBN: 978-1-4759-5768-6 (ebk)

Printed in the United States of America

iUniverse rev. date: 11/09/2012

This book is dedicated to Kievyn & Alondra,
the reasons for everything that I do

Contents

Acknowledgements

I would like to thank my mom for always encouraging me in everything that I've ever done. For listening to me over the years and always giving me great advice even if I didn't know at the time that it was great advice. I'd also like to thank her for reading and commenting on the final draft of this book; I know that must have been difficult for her. Whether we're 42 or 14, we are always going to be their babies.

I want to thank my friend Simone and my sister-in-law Soroya for listening to me talk on and on, vent, complain and break promises about every relationship that I've had in the last 15 years. Though their approaches and opinions were vastly different, each managed to listen without criticism or judgment and usually never made me feel stupid. They both gave good advice though it wasn't always realized immediately. There's nothing like girl talk to make you feel better.

Sean, when I need a reality check, you give it to me. You hold no punches and though your words and opinions are sometimes harsh, they're always on point. You make me look at things from an entirely different point of view and pull me up when I start to regress. Ours is an untraditional friendship but one that I cherish.

LT, you lit a fire under me when I almost gave up on this project. Thanks for the encouragement.

Last but never least, thanks to the Most High, Jah; where would I be without you watching over me?

Introduction

This is not a male-bashing book nor is it a manual on how to find, marry or keep a man. It's simply a documentation of one woman's journey to find love. Love, that seemingly possible yet usually unattainable thing we are raised to believe we will inevitably find. Not just love but the whole package; the house, the cars, the kids, the vacations, the PTA meetings and let's not forget, the hot sex every night. True, we're faced with the daunting statistics of high divorce rates, the probable infidelity of our men, the increasing acceptance of same-sex couples and the many who are jailed, under-educated and/or generally unfit to be called men. But most of us choose to look past those daunting statistics and focus on the task, the task of finding a man and living the dream. The lucky ones find him or some watered-down version fairly easily while the rest of us sift through the remnants. Wondering how and why we can't find someone who'll sweep us off our feet just like in the movies. Reality bites and we soon realize that Prince Charming isn't sitting outside our door on his white horse. After a while we're forced to remove our rose-colored glasses and reevaluate the list that we've had in our head for so long, that now seems over the top. You know the one that says:

1. MBA or PHD
2. 6-figure salary with good credit
3. 6 feet 2 inches, minimum
4. Drop dead gorgeous
5. Great in bed
6. Sensitive to my needs
7. Heterosexual
8. I could go on

So we cut back on some things and compromise; okay, he doesn't have to have an MBA as long as he's graduated college. Okay, so he's 5 feet 8 inches, I could wear my heels when I'm going out with the girls. We tell ourselves that we are strong women, we are independent and we can fix these men or *"train"* them to be exactly how we want them to be. Train them? I'm in awe of women who claim to be able to do this. I can't even train my poodle and I've had him for 6 years, almost as long as my husband. I still believe in the fairy tale and though my Prince Charming hasn't revealed himself yet, I refuse to become totally jaded.

They say that today, 1 in 6 relationships have started with online dating therefore there must be something to it; but I'm not there yet. I haven't reached the point of online or speed dating or any of those extreme measures but I totally respect those that put themselves out there like that. I admire a woman who can strike up a conversation with a man that they find attractive or to just have a chat with. A woman that can slip their phone number to someone or even ask them out on a date. Easy for some but not for me, even at this age I find that an amazing challenge. One day I'll do it though when I'm feeling particularly brave. I should be like my sister-in-law who within minutes of entering a club, bar or lounge will be surrounded by guys. Is it that she's drop-dead gorgeous or is it that she exudes an energy that says "*I'm drop-dead gorgeous and I know it.*" She's not afraid to speak first. Confidence is a hell of thing. It is so important and such an attractive quality, one that resonates from within and not easily faked. Faking it usually comes off as insecurity. I'm not sure one can learn to be confident, one can learn to look it but feeling it takes some work. That's something I'm still working on.

When I was about 2, my father moved back to Trinidad so I did not grow up with him as a constant presence in my life. I visited him often though, spending quite a few summers with him but we never really developed that father-daughter bond. I love him and I know that he loves me but I wonder what effect his absence had on me and my ability to form long-lasting relationships. He has four other children by three different women but I am the only child for my mother and I grew up an only child. I don't recall my mother having any boyfriends, if she did, they were not significant in my life or I have just blanked them out. My family was strict and my early years were pretty uneventful.

When I was fourteen, I got myself into trouble hanging out with a fast crowd smoking marijuana on a daily basis and skipping school, lots of school. How I made it through the ninth grade is still a mystery. I was living with my grandparents in Queens; eventually they found out about the smoking and missing school. They gave me a choice, either move to Brooklyn with my mother or to England with my aunt; I chose England. I spent two years there and the experience was life-changing. To this day I wish I had stayed there as I'm sure I would have ended up with a totally different and probably better life. England is a place where you can be yourself, at least that's the effect it had on me. I always felt at home there, free to be me. At age 16 I got homesick and returned to New York. I moved in with my mother who still lived in Brooklyn and enrolled in college.

Now I am a forty-two year old divorced mother of two living and working in New York. Considered pretty by most; tall, slim, educated, with a great career. So why can't I establish a loving, long-term relationship? What am I doing wrong? Is it me or is it them? That's what I need to find out. How does that saying go? Something about insane people doing the same thing over and over yet expecting a different outcome. I'm certainly not crazy but I find myself ending up in similar situations, time and time again.

I believe it's crucial to examine one's past in order to move into the future. When a relationship ends, it is very easy to blame the other person. Most people cannot admit their own faults and how they may have contributed to the demise of a relationship. It's always what the other person did or said or couldn't do. Even if the other person did something so terrible, so unforgivable, could there be something in the way that we projected ourselves that allowed them to even go there? That's why we should go through this process. The process of examining each relationship, to honestly look back and try to pinpoint what went wrong and why before venturing into the next. We often jump from one right into the next with little thought.

It's especially difficult when we discuss every aspect of our relationship with friends or family from the first date to the last goodbye, entertaining their commentary all the way. Yes, as women we are cursed with the need to talk about our feelings. It is what it is, that's how we handle things. We're Venusians, it's how we operate. But we don't always need the advice, sometimes we just need to vent and get it out of our system. Many times when I'm faced with a dilemma or just have the need to talk, I'll talk to myself out loud while driving just because I don't want to discuss the issue with anyone or I know they're fed up of hearing about it yet again. You'll be surprised how much better I feel having gotten the issue off my chest yet not having discussed another part of my relationship with someone other than the person I'm in the relationship with. By entertaining the advicc of others, we run the risk of making decisions based on *their* experiences and *their* point of views which may not be the same as ours. Also, we are more likely to subconsciously describe the issue in our favor and leave out crucial details. We tend to follow fashion because we're scared of what others might think.

I'm not taking him back! If I do, what will the girls think?

I'm learning to follow my gut, that whole women's intuition thing actually works sometimes. And if it doesn't, at least I can be satisfied knowing that I came to whatever decision on my own and not have that gut wrenching feeling of regret because it wasn't really what I wanted to do.

I have a very poor memory, especially for bad experiences. I tend to block them out and it drives me and other people crazy. Maybe it's a protective mechanism. So I have always kept journals; not writing everyday but trying at least to document significant events. There have been times that I've gone months without writing and when I go back to read my journals and see those gaps I'm devastated because I don't remember details and feelings. I find it so helpful to be able to go back and read about, for example, when I first met a guy, how I felt and how he treated me then follow the progression of the relationship through my own words. I've often written notes to myself like *"Don't forget how he treated you today. Don't forget how bad you feel right now!"* And true to form like the forgiving person that I am, when I read that, only then am I reminded of the incident and how it affected me. Long forgotten. So I try my best to keep to that practice and encourage all my friends to do the same.

It was by reading those very journals that I came upon the idea of writing this book. It was by reading those very journals that I started to see a pattern in myself. I was making the same questionable choices in men and hadn't, according to my own writings, learned anything. It was right in front of me, all of my mistakes. No, let me not call them that because those decisions were right for me at the time. Everything happens for a reason and people come into your life for a reason, a season or a lifetime as the saying goes. Sometimes I think we just tell ourselves that just to feel better about the dumb shit we do. I know there has to be a reason why I keep choosing guys that according to my sister-in-law "need fixing." What is it about me that needs to feel needed and how can I break the cycle? I've read *Men Are from Mars, Women Are from Venus* and found it very enlightening. I read *Act Like a Lady, Think Like a Man* and found it very informative. Yet here I am having not too long ended my significantly worst, most destructive relationship. It's time for a change and even if that means giving up the dream of that seemingly possible yet usually unattainable thing, I have to work on me. I deserve better and I have to start believing that.

Chapter 1

THE EARLY CONTENDERS

Between the ages of 17 and 19, I was partying every weekend and attending college during the week. I worked part time so I always had money having different jobs from day care center teacher to insurance agent clerk and received lots of male attention. For some reason though, even at that tender age, I was marriage minded. Not that I wanted to get married right then but I'd evaluate the guys that I met on that level. When I look back I wonder what the hell was the matter with me. I was supposed to just have fun but I always took things way too seriously.

Like most of my friends, I would meet guys at parties. I did not socialize at my community college so I never had the opportunity to meet anyone there. Meeting guys at parties, in the dark, was always scary because when the lights came on . . . wow! You just never knew. We'd usually exchange numbers; they would call then come to my house a few days later. I don't remember being wined or dined, maybe an occasional movie or drive to the beach. Technically it wasn't really dating was it? I was rarely taken on an actual date. My mom would always say that I should see more than one person at a time but that seemed so weird to me. None of my friends did that. She said I shouldn't settle or settle down. That was such good advice but I was too stupid to listen at the time. My aunt used to say *"Look for a guy with money. Go for the money girl!"* I found that so crass, used to think that's why she ended up single. She was so focused on finding someone with a degree or an education or a good job. My dumb ass would say to her *"I am looking for love."* Didn't I value myself enough to reach for the best? She'd say, *"It's just as easy to fall in love with someone with money, as it is to fall in love with someone without."* She was so right, it's actually easier.

I must mention my experience with molestation as it must have some influence on this issue. Having blocked out a lot of it, details are sketchy but to this day, I hate being held down. If you want to make me cry, hold me down on a bed with my wrists above my head and I will fucking lose it. I don't know when it started or when it stopped but I am thinking it stopped somewhere around age 12. It was a friend of the family who had moved in with us. He was very cute and I had a childhood crush on him. I must have blamed myself for it because this was someone I loved like an uncle but crushed on too. But please understand we're talking about the kind of crush an 8 year old has on someone. I remember trying not to be left alone with him though I am sure I was because there was no reason for me not to be. He never penetrated me but certainly fingered me and played with my undeveloped vagina. I don't recall any threats if I told, I just didn't tell. I think I wished he'd just stop so I could grow up and we could be married. When he did get married I was jealous of his wife but I was also scared for her daughter. Such confusing emotions.

Fast forward to age 18 and he's resurfaced. I'm torn because I can't forget what he did to me yet I'm still crushing on him. But he makes me nervous as hell. We hung out once or twice, why I don't know. He came to my house one day as I was getting ready for class, my mother was at work and I had just showered. I had on a robe. Don't know why I thought things could be different. I asked him to wait in the living room so I could get dressed but he came to the back bedroom anyway, pinned me up against the wall and asked me for a kiss. I resisted but like I said, I don't like to be restrained. I begged him to go.

"Just give me one kiss and I'll leave," he begged. So I kissed him. Big mistake.

"Who taught you to kiss like that? No way am I leaving now. I didn't know you could kiss like that?" he said.

We struggled for some time, my robe slipping open revealing my breasts which excited him even more. The phone rang which distracted him and allowed me to break away. I tried to stay on the phone as long as I could so that he could calm down. I don't know how but I convinced him to leave and vowed never to let myself be near him again. I still to this day wonder why I let him get near me, don't understand the control he had over me. It's a wonder that I can be intimate with men today without having undergone years of therapy.

Back to the dating game: I met a lot of guys, there was this one, he was Panamanian, sexy as hell and the sex was amazing. I don't think I had an orgasm until I was about 30 years old but he had me like a waterfall and to top it off, he spoke Spanish. I remember when I first saw him. I had a summer job at an insurance agency. He walked around like he knew he was the shit because he was. Dark skin, curly hair, he wore suits every day and you could see the shape of his body through them. I'm not much of a body girl, the muscles don't do it for me but it was working for him. I knew the minute I saw him that I wanted him but I didn't think for a moment that I could get him. He was obviously hit on by every girl in the office. When he smiled, oh Lord, his teeth were perfect and white. Somehow within a month, he was mine. Everything was great but two things turned me off and I knew it couldn't go any further. To me, at that time, if I couldn't see myself with you forever, you were a waste of time. First, he had a daughter which wasn't the problem. She was cute but when she smiled, her mouth turned up into a most unattractive position. There was no way I could chance that my child could end up like that. Second, he sweated too much. One night he came to pick me up, he must have come from work because he had on a suit and when he took off the jacket, there were large sweat stains under his arms. I mean large! He didn't smell but he was sweating like a pig. Do you know that's what ultimately did him in? I couldn't be with a man that sweated like that. I am telling you, I have issues.

There was this Chinese Jamaican guy that I met at a party; he looked so handsome in the dark but when he came to see me the next day I realized he had a mouth full of rotten teeth! Okay, maybe they were just slightly discolored. Why would a young guy allow his mouth to get like that? And he was so cute. What a waste. But what did I do? I fucked him anyway. Not the next day but eventually. Not to offend anyone of Oriental descent but I gotta tell you the truth, the rumors are true. What a waste of time, once was enough for me. Next!

I had a boyfriend that was a drug dealer. I actually liked him a lot but he had a lot of girls after him probably because it was cool to be with a dealer at the time. I guess it still is for some ladies but I really liked him. He had this way of walking that looked like he was walking sideways, it was so cute. We would go to a hotel, where else could we go? That was the scene back then. But I always felt dirty and never got out of the car until he got the keys to the room.

What if someone saw me in the lobby?

This was no fancy hotel in the city; it was a hotel on the service road of the Grand Central Pkwy which is still there today. The sex was monotonous and boring, I didn't know much then but I knew that wasn't the good stuff. My desire to be his girl kept me going back though. Days, weeks would go by and I wouldn't hear from him. I knew I was probably just one of many but my dumb ass jumped whenever he called. Eventually I wised up. I heard many years later that he was shot and killed; glad I wasn't around for that drama.

I dated an older Jamaica man, he was so sweet. I met him in a club in Manhattan and we just clicked. He was one of those goody-goody guys that would take off their jacket for you and open the car door. I could see in his eyes that he was serious but I was so young. Everything was going great until one day right after we made love; I sat up in the bed, looked at him and felt nauseous. I have no idea why that happened but that was it. It was never the same again and it was soon over.

The Rapper, yes I dated a rapper, a B-list but a rapper never the less. We met at The Red Parrot in Manhattan; he was infatuated with Slick Rick who is from England. I still had remnants of my English accent so he was instantly intrigued and since I was never one to dress overly sexy, he thought I stood out from the other girls who were dressed like they were next in line to work the pole. To make matters more interesting, I didn't know who the hell he was because his one hit song was hot when I was living in England. I had never even heard of this dude. We hit it off immediately though. The first time I went to visit him at his house; I took a cab which he paid for. He lived in the projects in Downtown Brooklyn, Fort Greene. Now keep in mind, even though I grew up in LeFrak City which some may consider hood, when my family moved in we were one of the first Black families. There was nothing hood about it though there was a time during the 'crack years' that things got a bit crazy. I had no prior experience with the projects so it was an adventure for me. I was attending New York City Technical College which wasn't far from his apartment so I would visit either after or before classes. We would have sex, my first taste of a big dick, then go out to eat or just hang out by him. One day, I showed up with a pair of yellow shoes and a yellow sweater that I had purchased in London; he kept going on and on about how nice I looked so he dressed up just like me. So there we were heading to Junior's for lunch both in yellow sweaters and shoes, I thought that was so cute. He was so excited to do that, for us to dress alike. That is my fondest memory of him. But he soon did something that caused all the fun to end. One day we were hanging out in his apartment, we just finished having sex when his DJ came by. He introduced me as "a friend." I was floored! I just finished sucking his dick and I'm a friend? That was pretty much the last time I saw him. Looking back, I know that I was totally wrong. We had had no conversation about being committed or exclusive; we weren't even calling each other boyfriend and girlfriend. What did I think was going to happen? That he would move me into the projects with him and we would live happily ever after? And he lived with his mother. Why do women do that? Assume that because you're having sex with someone, that you're automatically in a relationship?

Then there was the much-older guy. He owned the fabric store that my mom shopped in and always flirted with me way before I was old enough for it to be considered appropriate. I don't remember how I ended up going out with him but I'm sure he asked me when I came into the store without my mom. He owned quite a few buildings and had a nice house. He also had a daughter and an ex-wife. After the young guys I had been with, I told myself that this old guy was gonna rock my world!

Yeah right.

After a few dates that involved hanging out at his house and not doing much else, he took me to an apartment in one of his buildings. It was obvious that this was the night that it was going to happen. He was gonna show me what real sex was, what it was like to really get down. This fool was such a disappointment. He was clueless! When it was over, I lay there totally unsatisfied, confused and disappointed. When he got up, he roughly stuck a paper towel between legs for me to clean up. Wow, really? That was the first and last time with him.

I try not to regret the choices I've made or the guys that I met over the years. I tell myself that I've learned something from each one and the next one will be 'The One.' I wait for my Prince Charming who is coming to sweep me off my feet. Who knew I'd have to go through all these frogs first?

Chapter 2

MY BABY DADDY

I was about 19 when I met him; he was 7 years older than I. He was the cousin of one of my best friends, Lisa. By this time, I didn't like to meet guys that didn't come with a referral, you know, at least one person that knew them and could give me somewhat of a background story. Not that it guaranteed anything but I thought it was better than meeting total strangers. I had gotten burned too many times already and was cautious.

So Baby Daddy (BD), I met at a club. His dad was a big party promoter at that time; he gave most of the major Trinidadian parties in Brooklyn. BD was tall, 6 feet 3 inches, good looking and physically fit. We danced, we exchanged numbers and the usual phone calls and hanging out took place. There was only one problem with BD, which was his mustache and hair. He had a mustache like Lionel Richie, you know the kind that grows down past the lips, heading to the chin but never quite making it? He also had an outdated hairstyle, sort of curly and long in the back, short in the front like a mullet. I don't know how I did it but I somehow convinced him to cut both. What a difference, now he had potential.

BD had a son, a baby boy and he had just broken up with the mother, according to him. They used to live together but I believed they were still having sex when we met though he denied it but he said that he wanted very much to get away from her. I was just what he needed to do that.

BD was well endowed and he was one of the first guys to go down on me. He was a ladies man for sure and very experienced. I don't know why he liked me but I was damn sure glad he did because the sex was great. This one day I went over his house, yes, he was back living with his parents and siblings; it was summertime and hot as hell. I knew we were going to have sex because we did every chance we got and like most young girls, I was always nervous about how I tasted. So I ran to bathroom to wash up but I couldn't find anything, not a rag or any soap so I looked in the medicine cabinet and the only thing I could find was rubbing alcohol. You guessed it; I wiped my vagina with alcohol thinking "*now it's really clean*". I went back to the bedroom, so excited, couldn't wait for his mouth to do what it was so good at. When he started to kiss my neck and move down to my breasts and then my belly, I thought I would explode right then. He slowly parted my thighs and began to tease my clitoris with his tongue then . . . . he looked up and said "You taste funny, what did you put down there?"

"Nothing," I said feeling so embarrassed that I did something so stupid and of course he wasn't going to go back down there so now I was embarrassed *and* pissed. What the fuck was I thinking? Youth is a hell of a thing.

After a few months of us being together, BD introduced me to his son who was now about one year old. He was so cute and I could have seen myself having his child. He and the mother weren't getting along, she was much older and apparently the jealous type. I was glad, the more they fought, the better I looked.

I got along really well with his family and loved spending time at their house. Unlike my family, they were loud and fun and their house was always full of people. Food was always cooking and famous entertainers were in and out of the house since his dad was a popular party promoter. But BD hated them. Well, hate is a strong word but he clearly did not like to be there for too long. Not me, I couldn't get enough, it was so exciting for me. Everything up until to this point had been great, we were happy and I had no reason to doubt that we would be together forever.

After about a year into the relationship, I noticed that I was spitting constantly. It was the weirdest thing. I wasn't nauseous and hadn't missed my period but just couldn't stop spitting. I soon found out that I was pregnant. I couldn't tell my mother, she would surely kill me. I was 20 years old and in my 3rd year of college, I only worked part time and didn't know what the hell to do. I told BD and he wasn't the slightest bit upset. He had no problem with me keeping the baby but as much as he wanted to, I knew I wasn't ready. I loved children, always had someone's child around me, had several God-children but this wasn't the right time. I decided to terminate, went all by myself. Took a taxi home and vowed to start taking birth control.

I started taking the Pill and within three days, I developed pains in my calf. Since blood clots were a side effect of the Pill, I had to stop immediately. A few months later, just before my 21st birthday, I got pregnant again. My dad was visiting from Trinidad at the time; he came up for my 21st birthday party. I couldn't hide it, I had to tell them. I sat down and told both my parents and they begged me not to have the baby. They convinced me that I was almost done with school and had plenty of time to have kids and that I should live my life. My dad took me down to this mega huge abortion clinic and I threw away yet another child. This time, I took it super hard. I tried another kind of the birth control pill but experienced similar side effects. I told BD that he would have to use condoms but he refused. He said it didn't feel the same with them on. Red Flag! Looking back, this is where I should have walked away; this was the point of no return.

Three months later, I was pregnant again. This time, I told my mom I was keeping my baby. She flipped out! She was driving when I told her this and all of a sudden she mashed down the accelerator and started driving like 80 mph. I told her to let me out; she could kill herself if she wanted. When we got home she made me call every one of my uncles, aunts and grandparents to tell them that I was pregnant which I did but let me tell you, they cried like I was 15 years old. I didn't understand at the time why they were so upset. I was 21, a few months from graduation and I already had a job lined up. I thought I had it all figured out. BD was happy, I was excited to be a mom and everything was going to be great. I thought I was in love; we'd get married, buy a house, two cars and live happily ever after. Or so I thought.

Fast forward to the summer of '91 and I was in the last trimester of my pregnancy. I graduated from college but I decided not to start working until I had the baby and I was nesting like a mother fucker. BD lost his job and fell into what I would call a deep depression. He started drinking way more than ever, hanging out all the time and being a general asshole. Of course I, like a true Scorpio, faced the problem head on. I tried to talk to him, to motivate him but at the end of the day, it was really all about me and the baby. So I started to withdraw, this is what I do when I'm backed into a corner. I went to Atlantic City almost every weekend with my mom and Granny just to get away. I sipped Perrier and lime, pulled the slots to pass the time and plotted my next move.

My friend Lisa approached me one day with some very interesting information about BD. She told me point blank that she had seen him with this particular girl on several occasions, her sitting on his lap even. I doubted her at first but I listened and digested the news. She came back to me the following week with more information. I couldn't just ignore it so again I decided to face the problem head on. I called him over and asked him directly if he was seeing someone else. Was he cheating on me, fucking another woman, having a fling?

Let's talk about it I said. You're busted so please don't waste my time trying to lie, let's just talk it out.

The asshole watched me in my face and told me that the girl was his cousin and that Lisa obviously didn't like me for her to tell me this when I was 8 months pregnant. I didn't know what to do; I couldn't go to the club to see for myself with my huge belly. So I withdrew from him even more. I wanted to believe him but why would Lisa lie? She wouldn't, I felt so confused.

The next month, I passed my due date and I was trying everything to jump start the labor. It was time for the Labor Day Parade in Brooklyn and since I couldn't join the revelers I decided to help BD's family sell food along Eastern Parkway. I figured standing up all day would have to start something going. The day was going great, the weather was beautiful, all my friends passed by to say hello and I was having fun with his family. I was just having a great time until he passed by the booth with a young woman and little girl. He walked up to the booth with the little girl on his shoulders. His mom muttered under her breath, "What is he doing with that red bitch?" All of a sudden, it's like I got hit by a ton of bricks and everything clicked into place. I felt sick to my stomach and I just knew that all that I heard was true. I felt it, knew it. I had seen the girl before; she lived next door to them. She was avoiding my stare and he was acting like nothing was wrong. I walked over to him and calmly asked him, "*What are you doing? Where are you going?*" I don't even remember what he said but eventually they left together, left me there with my 9½ month belly looking like a total ass. Somehow I got through the day and went back to his family's house after the parade. His family was visibly pissed at him and they told me that she had been sleeping there with him on the floor for a while.

Now you tell me?

I said nothing, I did nothing. In my mind it was over, not because he cheated but because he lied to my face. The trust was gone and once that's gone, what's left? I went home and finished preparing for the birth of my child.

When I finally went into labor, I called him; he came to the hospital and sat next to me listening to his Walkman while I was writhing in pain. No epidural for me. He dozed off and on and eventually I told his sorry ass to get the fuck out and send my mother in. By now she had calmed down considerably and was actually excited to be a grandmother. I gave birth to a beautiful 9 pound 9 ounce baby boy who almost ripped me in half. I was expecting a girl so I had no name prepared; thank God I bought everything for the baby in yellow and green. I struggled to think of a name so BD came up with something suitable. I gave the baby his last name because, because . . . well I'm not really sure why but I figured child support would be easier and just in case he ever made something of himself, I would make sure my son carried his name. It made sense at the time. I never even filed for support.

We went through the motions over the next few months; we christened the baby, showed him off to the entire family but our relationship really just revolved around our son. I was getting ready to start my new job and BD was still not working. I asked him what he may possibly contribute; maybe he could stay home with the baby so I could save on babysitting. He refused. Then, when our son was about three months old, BD said that New York was over for him. He couldn't find work and he didn't want to be around his family so he was moving to Georgia. He wanted the baby and me to come.

No way. I am contractually committed to this job for a minimum of two years plus I don't want to go anywhere with you!

So he went without us saying maybe we'll join him later. We never did.

Old Years Night—BD was gone, my son just made three months and I decided that this was a perfect time to start fresh. I would bring in the New Year at Lisa's house, she was having a party. I met this gorgeous man; his smile was so perfect and he was such a gentleman though just a little shorter than me. We danced all night and fantasized about what could be.

Umm, excuse me; didn't you just have a baby?

Okay, back to reality. We exchanged numbers but I knew what I had waiting at home, a beautiful baby boy.

Later on that month I got a phone call from BD; he said that his "friend" was moving down to Georgia; the same girl that he cheated on me with. I was devastated, relieved, hurt and kind of happy all at the same time. Once I found out he lied, the relationship was never the same for me. Good riddance, I thought, his loss. I'm sure I cried but my tears were soon erased by a smile from my little boy. In true fashion, I dusted myself off and moved on the Next!

What have I learned?

I obviously missed the warning signs: his reluctance to wear condoms was crucial since I could not use birth control. He still lived with his mother, he had just come out of a serious relationship and he had a young baby. Those issues by itself should have been enough for me to take things very slowly, to not start a serious relationship or to just say, this is not what I'm looking for. I was way too young to get myself caught up in such a situation, I should have kept it moving but at least one very important thing came out of it; my son.

Chapter 3

COULD WOULDA SHOULDA

This is the guy that I met on Old Year's Night (New Year's Eve). Let's refer to him as Shorty from here on in. It was January 1992 and we had been talking on the phone a lot but I made it clear to him that my baby's dad just had moved out of state and I didn't know where we stood. He was okay with that; he was so patient and such a gentleman that it blew me away. By the way, he was Trinidadian too. Once I found out that the girl had moved down to Georgia to be with BD, I decided it was time to really move on but I was in no rush to jump into a physical relationship with someone new.

Over the next few months, Shorty and I did everything together and spent every available moment with each other. He got along with my family, I got along with his. He had a son who lived in another state so there were no issues there. Shorty was like a father to my son; he was my man and I was stupid over him. Still no sex had taken place.

He had a fairly decent job but said he got fired from a really good job right before we met. He'd been attending college but dropped out and I was trying to get him to go back. He had this soft demeanor and was by no means a take-charge kind of guy which was frustrating at times. Shorty showed so much potential hence the name Coulda Woulda Shoulda. Still lived at home but he had the basement apartment with a separate entrance so at least we had privacy. He hung out a lot but not excessively and his friends were my best friend's friends so it was always fun and familiar. Shorty was athletic, played basketball regularly and was generally thought of as the good guy amongst the crew. The responsible one, as was I to my friends.

September 1992—After nine long months we finally decided that it was time to seal the deal. Now of course we had messed around a bit but we never had sex up until now and we were hell bent on making it special. I couldn't wait! My son was with my mom and we were in his basement apartment. We burned incense, drank wine and smoked some weed. We took our time, no ripping of clothes or throwing down like wild beasts though after nine months one might be inclined to do that. No, we drank and smoked and built up the anticipation. We kissed and caressed each other, told each other how much love we had for one another. The heat continued to build and I was ready, so ready. No one can say I jumped from man to man and for that I was so proud of myself. I slid off his pants ready to get busy but he was not quite hard. I was confused. Why was he not bursting through his pants? Okay, I tried to stimulate him, slowly, teasing, biting, trying everything to get a response but nothing, nada, zilch. Frustration, anger and embarrassment set in. Why was I embarrassed? I turned to him for an explanation; he said it was the anticipation, the buildup mixed with the weed and liquor. I got no loving that night but lots of hugs and kisses and *I love yous*. A different kind of loving.

A couple of days later, without the big prelude, we managed to seal the deal and it was all good. I mean, I was sure *this* was the man for me. I was sure we would have gotten married and lived happily ever after. We got along so well, we never fought, and I had genuine love for this man. Then . . . he lost his job. He felt defeated and was unable to really dig in and muster up any kind of motivation or determination. His attitude toward us remained the same, but his overall attitude was like *woe is me, woe am I*. It was such a turnoff but I loved him and I was determined to fix everything. He looked for a job but was only met with rejection. To make matters worse, I was working as a RN and making a good salary. One day he came over and told me that he and his best friend were going to Texas to look for work. I was floored. I felt like I got hit in the chest.

What the fuck do you mean you're going to Texas? Lubbock, Texas has a job for you and New York doesn't? Are you retarded?

He told me that he was a man and had to do what he could to make a way for our family. He professed his undying love for us and I believed him but begged him not to go. He went anyway. I was just about to turn 23 when this happened.

We kept in touch, talked almost every day but it wasn't the same. I went back to hanging out with the girls and of course, what do you think happened? I met a guy; let's call him Dexter because I always associate this name with a man that has a big enough dick and ego to sling over his shoulder. Now Dexter had a girlfriend and technically I had a boyfriend but I was loving his personality. He was fun and upbeat and loved to fuck! Yes, he was a Trinidadian too. Are you starting to see a pattern? We were enjoying each other, just having fun, no mention of a relationship or where it was going because it obviously wasn't going anywhere. Just fun and sex and laughs. One day Dexter was hanging out at my house, sitting on the sofa. We must have been getting ready to go out, my mom was home at the time and we heard a knock at the door. I looked through the peephole and guess who was at the door? Shorty! I let him in. What was I going to do, leave him out there?

"What are you doing here? When did you get back to New York?" I asked.

He wanted to surprise me, he missed us so much. I felt like a pack of shit. So there's Dexter on the couch, not moving and Shorty standing there wondering who the other guy is. Shorty soon put two and two together and said he would leave. I didn't want him to leave, I wanted Dexter to get the fuck up and get the fuck out but he just sat there. I didn't know what to do; I didn't want to offend either person. Eventually Shorty walked out the door; the look on his face killed me. Now I was pissed at Dexter. I asked him to leave.

"Why didn't you go when you saw my boyfriend come back?" I screamed.

Now he was playing dumb. How did I get myself in those situations?

Shorty and I talked the next day and he admitted that it wasn't fair of him to leave me especially when everything was going so well. He said didn't blame me for seeking attention from someone else. I promised to end all contact with Dexter and we decided to pick up where we left off. Despite me being happy that Shorty was back, things weren't quite the same but I pushed on. Soon Shorty got a job and a few months later we moved in together in May of 1993. This was the first time that I left home to venture out on my own. We rented a two-bedroom apartment in Canarsie, Brooklyn and had the best time decorating it and living as a family. We did everything together and it seemed all the back to the way it was before he left for Texas. I was 23, my son was twenty months old and we were so happy; I am again convinced that we will be together forever.

Fast forward to February 1994, I decided to go Trinidad for Carnival. Shorty did not want to go; I took my son with me. I went with two friends, Jenny and her sister Paula that were both older than me. I always had older friends, not sure why. Jenny, who was 34, was seeing a guy who lived in Trinidad who was 21. Okay. The night before I left, Shorty and I had a romantic evening together since I would have been in Trinidad for Valentine's Day. Before I left the house for the airport, I pasted hearts all over the wall above our bed and left chocolates and a card for him. I wanted to make sure he thought about me the entire time as I would have been thinking about him. I was totally content with this man, we were happy, we were a family.

Jenny's boyfriend picked us up at the airport; him and his friend. They were driving a pick-up truck. His friend, James, had that look that made me weak. I couldn't stop staring at him and I noticed him looking at me too.

What's wrong with me? Didn't I leave a good man at home?

Over the next two weeks James and I continued flirting and hanging out together, by the end of the vacation, we were in love. We went to the beach, fooled around in the Botanic Gardens, drank Puncheon Rum in a local bar and talked about everything. When it was time for me to leave, we were both damn near in tears. We promised to write to each other, keep in touch and to hopefully be together one day. He gave me a pair of his shorts that I loved on him and I gave him a tee shirt of mine that he loved on me. I am telling you, if I could have stayed in Trinidad at that moment with him, I would have. That's how gone I was.

The night I arrived home, Shorty was so happy to see me but my response was lukewarm. Of course he picked up on it right away and gave me a look like he knew something was wrong. I tried to fake it but I just couldn't. The very night I got back, I sat down on the steps and began to tell him what happened in Trinidad. I told him that I met someone and got a little caught up but that I was over it and over the guy. He was upset, of course but very understanding which made me feel even worse. He was a really good guy. I told myself that what happened in Trinidad wasn't real and what the hell was I gonna do, move down there? Move James up here? I tried to get back into the relationship but then, James called.

He called me every day and I called him every night. We wrote each other and James wrote love letters like no one else could. All this was unknown to Shorty of course. I talked to my friends, Jenny and Paula, about my feelings for James and his for me. They were both skeptical figuring James just wanted to find a way to get to come to America. Paula said that he didn't have a pot to piss in or a window to throw it out of. This touched a nerve with me and I started to panic.

What if he just using me?

I told James what they said and he reassured me that his love was real but I continued throwing doubt on his words. Meanwhile Shorty was trying his best to be Superman. Little did I know he was still suspicious the entire time.

One afternoon I was in my bedroom talking on the phone to James; I thought I was alone in the house. Suddenly

Shorty jumped out of the closet. Busted! He went ballistic. He couldn't believe I was still talking to the guy. After this incident things got really tense and he wouldn't leave me alone for one minute. Every evening I rushed to the mailbox because I knew the phone bill was coming. Why hadn't it come yet? Then I found out that Shorty intercepted the bill and was hiding it. $350! With about 30 calls to Trinidad. This couldn't go on, didn't make any sense. Shorty and I decided to part ways. I planned to move back to my mom's and he would live out the rest of the lease. When I told James this, he told me that he had gotten back together with his old girlfriend since I didn't believe that he loved me. So now I had lost both men.

Shorty promised to remain part of my son's life since he was the only father he'd ever known but he didn't. We hardly ever saw each other and when we did it was uncomfortable. James and I stopped speaking and my girlfriends were only too happy. I read his letters every so often and keep them tucked away in a special box. After a few months I was ready to move on. I got an apartment in Brooklyn for my son and me and decided to stay single for a while. That was until October of that same year.

What have I learned?

Looking back, I can say that I was probably too young to have moved in with a man. I had never lived on my own or had a chance to discover who I was. Even though I took it very, very slow, I cheated on him and despite the fact that he forgave me and gave me another chance, I obviously wasn't ready. This was one relationship where I can say that I was totally to blame for it coming to an end. I could blame some of it on him and say that him moving to Texas when things were going so well caused me to drift away but chances are, I would have done it anyway.

Chapter 4

THE CORRECTION OFFICER?

October 1994, carnival time in Miami. Some friends and I were heading down for a few days. It was party after party and cuties from all over were in town. I met this guy; let's call him Frank after Frank Abagnale. He had real lyrics, you know what I mean? He made himself seem very important and of course, he got my attention. Not super good looking, he was actually kind of on the chunky side, his belly could have used some deflation but it was a flirty weekend so I was playing along. We exchanged numbers right away which I don't usually do especially since I didn't know anyone who knew him. I figured he would lose it and we weren't in New York but the mister called me constantly when we got back to Brooklyn.

Now, I had yet to introduce anyone to my son except for Shorty and I was hesitant about it. I figured he shouldn't meet anyone unless we were serious so I kept little man away. From the first time Frank came to visit, the man took over. His presence was just so overwhelming and I lost my voice to speak up and say no. First of all, I knew nothing about this dude except what he told me. He said he had a son though I had never seen a picture nor did he ever speak about him, as most parents do. He said his ex-girlfriend was the daughter of the owner of one of the most popular Trinidadian restaurants in Brooklyn. We hardly ever went out, I had never met any of his friends, he just came over and we had sex but somehow this guy was calling the shots. He insisted that we find a babysitter for my son so that when he needed to come over, we could have some private time. Red Flag! That was the turning point, that was when I should have said, no thanks, you're not the one for me. The nerve of this dude but did I say anything? Nope, I just sat there as he went on and on. Every so often he pulled a disappearing act, not answering his pages and not calling for days. Once after a few days of not hearing from him, he finally called and said he'd been on lock-down at Riker's Island. You see, he was supposed to be a correction officer which is why he always carried a gun. The lock-down, he explained, happened because a prisoner tried to escape and the remaining prisoners started rioting. They were forbidden to leave the island until control was restored. I never asked why this event didn't make the news. Another time he showed up at my house with one those papers from the shooting range. You know the one with the outline of the man with bullet holes in it? He was so happy because he scored the highest in his group; apparently they were tested every so often. Now, this certainly proved that he was a correction officer, right?

Soon after I had moved into my apartment, my brother showed up at my door; his girlfriend had thrown him out. He asked to stay for two weeks but ended up staying permanently. Now, he knew Frank from playing ball in the park and he was very suspicious of his stories. He said he'd never heard of him being a correction officer and as far as he knew he was married to the girl that he said was his ex-girlfriend. Why didn't I listen to my brother? I mean, he was out there and wouldn't lie about something like that, not my own brother. But somehow in my mind, I told myself that he was wrong. I didn't even like Frank all that much but I seemed to have this need not to be wrong and a need to have a man.

The phone rang one night; it was one of my dearest friends, Cathy. She was also older than me as most of my friends were. She was very upset and proceeded to tell me in the most concerning voice that I should run from Frank. That he was lying about everything and someone who was at her house was telling her all this because she had mentioned who my boyfriend was. I was so confused but also a bit angry. Instead of listening to her, I told her that her friend was wrong and that all was well with us. Looking back now, I must have been out of my damn mind. How many Red Flags did I need?

The relationship lasted 1 year from start to finish. I told myself that I would stay with him until someone better came along. I hadn't met anyone new so I figured it was better to have someone than to have no one at all. In retrospect, I was developing a very needy disposition that many women fall victim to. One day he told me that he had an offer to play professional football in Trinidad, some minor league. Football? I had never even seen this dude watch a football game nevertheless play good enough to be recruited by another country. Over the next few weeks he was pretty distracted with making the decision about whether to leave or stay and wanted to know if I would come with him.

Why is someone always trying to take me away?

He decided to go but by the time he left for Trinidad the relationship was pretty much dead. After hearing even more people voice their concerns about him and his false stories, I eventually lost interest.

I decided then to make it a practice to sit and think about every relationship I'd had. I asked myself what went wrong. What did *I* do wrong? Were there any warning signs that I ignored? I promised myself that the next time would be different, that I didn't need a man to feel fulfilled but I was lying to myself because that's not how I truly felt. By now I was 25 and I had subconsciously set certain goals for myself which needed to be met by a particular age. College degree by 21, marriage and first house by 25, 2 children by 30; I should have already been married by now according to the plan. I imagined my life like a hill that's really steep on one side with 25 at the top. Once I reached the top, the hill went down on the other side but not as steeply; it was all downhill from there. So, at 25, I was going through what was the equivalent of a mid-life crisis. I was freaking out because I wasn't even close to getting married, I had 5 more years to have my second child and my dream house was nowhere in sight. I didn't know it then but this was a turning point for me and instead of realizing how wrong I was to feel that way, I continued to make bad decision after bad decision.

What have I learned?

So many lessons to be learned here from knowing a liar when you see one to understanding how devaluing yourself can lead you to make poor decisions. From knowing its okay to be single, to be alone but not be lonely to listening to that inner voice that tells you when something isn't right. From listening to the people around you who obviously see what you sometimes can't to just taking your time to grow and learn to love yourself. If I had the self-confidence and the common sense at 25 to know that my outlook on life was so illogical, who knows where I would have been today. But I didn't and though I promised myself to make better decisions; I sat perched with trepidation at the top of that imaginary hill.

Chapter 5

THE ONE THAT I MARRIED

Now we've reached the end of the summer of 1995; I was hanging out as usual, my little man was with me. He was just about to turn 4 and full of energy. I was in the company of two young men, one who looked kind of scruffy; they were talking about their upcoming trip to Miami carnival in a couple of months and were discussing renting a car for the trip and other details. I don't know why but I was drawn to the scruffy one but puzzled as to what the attraction was. Nothing transpired that day but the following week Paula called to ask me if I would rent a car for her friend to use in Miami; it was the same guy, the scruffy one. Now, normally this request would have been met with an "*Are you out of your fucking mind?*" but I actually considered it. Why, I have no clue. She said she would get back to me after she spoke with him again. I asked about him, you know, for a referral and she had nice things to say but said he was young. How young she wasn't sure but younger than me. It didn't sway my curiosity.

The next week or so later, Paula invited me to a Sweet 16 party of a mutual acquaintance, Scruffy would be there she mentioned. Of course I jumped at the opportunity so I could get a really good look at him. Paula and I went to the Sweet 16 together and it was a big to do, like a wedding. I saw the guy that I had met with the scruffy one a few weeks earlier. He was front and center and I soon figured out he was the boyfriend of the girl who was celebrating her birthday and the scruffy one was her best friend. But where was he? All of a sudden, I felt eyes on me. I looked to my right and there he was standing right next to me but he was not scruffy tonight. He'd cut his hair, had on a tux and he was looking sweet. Of course I tried to seem uninterested. We talked and danced but were playing it cool with each other. He didn't ask for my number but I knew I'd see him again.

As I waited for him to track me down, I started my investigation. Cathy's daughter Maria, who was more my age, her boyfriend knew Scruffy, so I went to her for information. I asked her if she knew him and she said, *"Who? That stupid boy?"* I would find out over the years that this was a typical response for Maria, she was a straight hater. Maria went on to tell me that Scruffy and her boyfriend actually grew up together and she thought he was about 17 years old. 17? Damn, jailbait. Apparently, her boyfriend's dad was some type of gangster back in the day and several young men lived in his home over the years, all doing some sort of illegal activity. RED FLAG! Here's where I should have said, thanks for the information and exit stage left. But not me; I pressed on.

Then Paula called me to ask if I could still rent the car for him but I wondered why he hadn't called to ask me himself. I asked Paula again what she knew about him and she insisted that he was a good person and was 'well off.' Now my interest piqued again. Eventually he did call and ask himself; I agreed but failed to tell him that I didn't even know if I had enough on my credit card to do so but I wanted to get to know him and that seemed like a good way.

I decided to go down to Miami for carnival with Cathy and Maria, Scruffy was supposed to arrive the next day. Somehow I end up sleeping on the floor since our hotel room wasn't as big as it was supposed to be. When Scruffy came to our room to pick me up to get the car and saw that I was sleeping on the floor; he told me to bring my bags.

And I did. Why, I don't know. I didn't really know this man but something just felt right. We went to the rental agency and of course my card got declined but he had money. I realized then that whole car rental thing was just a way to meet me. We checked into his hotel, a really swanky place on the upper end of Collins Avenue. How did I end up here? We spent the next few days together, getting to know each other. No hanky panky, not even a kiss; we even slept in separate beds. I missed my flight to go home so he bought me ticket on his flight so we could fly home together. So began the courtship.

The first time he came to visit me at my apartment, he pretty much never left. He just stayed. Still no sex, he just stayed. He currently lived with his mother, sister, brother and nephew in a studio apartment and slept on the couch. He had just turned 20 the month before we met and though he was not the oldest child he was certainly the man of the house. That was the thing about him that attracted me; he was young but old in spirit. He didn't wear sneakers or jeans, he didn't drink or smoke and had a way about him that commanded respect yet he managed to be childish at the same time. He got along really well with my son and I got along well with his family. My friends couldn't really understand how we got so close so fast. Maria and Cathy were convinced that I was under a spell, actually they thought his mom was working Obeah on me but I was happy and once again thought I had met *The One*. He didn't have a 9-5; he was a hustler all the way. But he didn't sell drugs or rob people; he was the guy who you could get you a flight to China for half the price. I knew this was wrong and a bad idea but I also felt that it was a temporary situation.

He knew that to be with me he would have to give up that life. He was intelligent and resourceful and I was convinced my influence on him would save him from his upbringing. Hustling was all he really knew prior to meeting me.

After 2 years of a damn near perfect relationship, the issue of his permanent residency came up. You see, he had been brought here from Trinidad by his mom for a visit when he was about 15 and was forced to stay. He was here illegally and the government was hacking down on illegal immigrants at that time. There was a new law passed that anyone who filed for a green card after a certain date would be required to return to their country and wait during the processing of the papers which could take up to 4 years. We got nervous so we decided that since we were eventually going to get married anyway, we might as well do it now. We got married in a civil ceremony with my son as the witness then moved from Brooklyn back to Queens. I was 27, he was 22 and it was 1997.

I was married and very happy. I just completed my Bachelor's degree and was preparing to start my Master's. Still trying to get him to go to college, to start the application for the green card and get a legitimate job. His hustling was by no means paying the bills or allowing us to live lavishly. As a matter of fact, I wouldn't allow us to incur any expenses that I couldn't afford on my paycheck. Somewhere deep, deep inside I knew that one day he would have to pay for it all so I had to make sure that I could afford to live without him. Anything that he brought in was excess, play-money per se. If I was smarter I would have banked it or at least stashed it..

A couple of years into the marriage, I got pregnant and was so happy because I was well within my time-line. My next goal to reach, in addition to my second child, was a house. We started looking right away and found something pretty quickly. For sure, I was the driver of this vehicle pushing for the house, the baby and for him to start school. I thought I had it all under control. He was very easy going and just happy to have a stable home as he had not had that growing up; he just let me make all the decisions.

Once we moved into the house, we didn't have much time to get settled because I was due to give birth in a few months. I spent most of the time focusing on getting the children's room and his office ready. I wanted the basement to be renovated into a play area for the children and an entertainment out area for our friends but we didn't have enough time or money to get it done right then. It was also very important to me that he didn't conduct any illegal activities from our home as his business involved using the Internet and was therefore traceable. I explained to him that this was our home, our children's home and I didn't want it defiled. I really wanted him to stop but I knew he wouldn't so I asked him to at least keep it far away from me. He promised he would but I would find out later that he didn't keep his promise.

One day as I headed down to the basement to do the laundry, I was surprised to see his brother Louis painting the walls. First I thought my husband was surprising me by fixing up the basement but according to Louis, he was going to be renting my basement for him and his 19 year old pregnant girlfriend! I stayed calm and asked what the arrangement was; $500 a month. Why yell at Louis, this was not his fault. I was in my last month of pregnancy and had already stopped working, what was I gonna do, leave? I had to deal with it. Hopefully it would only be temporary and at least we'd have extra income coming in.

Our daughter was born in December of 1999, we were ecstatic. Two months later, Louis and his now wife, were a few weeks from the birth of their child and I got another surprise. Their mother, Louis and my husband's, was moving in to help the girl with their baby as she was so young. Okay. There were upsides to this arrangement as she would also help me cook and clean but I still wasn't happy. Hopefully her presence would be temporary also.

Over the next year and a half we all lived together in our 3 bedroom house, though I never saw a penny of rent from anyone. My husband continued to conduct his business from his laptop, often sneaking to do it in the middle of the night and we argued about it all the time. I would catch him when I got up to check on the baby or to use the bathroom. He insisted that he had ways of making sure he wasn't tracked. I made sure I tripled my life insurance and kept my maiden name.

One summer day while I was out shopping, I got a frantic call from Cameron, my daughter's godfather and my husband's best friend. Apparently our home had been invaded by the Secret Service and I was instructed to get home immediately and not drive our Lexus SC400 onto the block. The only thing on my mind was my daughter as she was home with them. I raced home and thanked God that my son was in Georgia with his dad. He would have been old enough to understand had he seen the agents ransacking the house; my daughter was only a year and half. I got home and my house looked like an episode from CSI; everything was tossed. I grabbed my daughter and demanded to know what the fuck was going on. The officers, one playing good cop and the other bad, proceeded to tell me that they knew I was not involved but that they had been tracking the fool, my husband, for a long time. They confiscated our computers, my Palm Pilot and files. They promised to return with a warrant for his arrest and the bad cop promised to return for me. I was beyond done. Part of me was thankful because I was thinking; now he'll stop but he didn't.

A few weeks later on September 11, the World Trade Center was attacked and the incident convinced my then husband that since the Secret Service building went down in flames, all the evidence against him was destroyed, therefore he was in the clear. He actually continued his activities in the house using another laptop. Like a true Scorpio, I hatched a plan. I put the house up for sale, it sold quickly and we had weeks to move. My plan was to lay low and regroup then start fresh again in a new home. Hopefully I could get him to stop in the interim otherwise; I was fully prepared to go it alone.

Moving day approached and he informed me that he wasn't moving, that he was going to Miami for carnival. He didn't believe I sold the house, he thought I was bluffing. Okay.

When he came back from Miami, the house was empty except for his clothes and the fridge.

I decided to rent a 4-bedroom apartment, moving his sister and her son in with us so that we could all save money but by then the marriage was strained. We had money in the bank from the sale of the house but his business wasn't going well and he was getting frustrated. He took half of our proceeds from the sale of the house for God knows what. He actually demanded it in the bank, in front of the teller saying that half belonged to him. Okay. Then one afternoon when we least expected it, there was a knock at the door. The good cop walked in calmly and quietly and told him it was time to go. That was it. There was no bail to post, just lawyers to be paid; this was a Federal case. He was sentenced to 33 months and would be deported back to Trinidad after time served. I was left in debt and alone to raise two kids but I had no one to blame but myself.

What did I learn?

The lessons here are obvious. You cannot save someone, at least not someone that doesn't want to be saved. You have to set standards for yourself and stick to them no matter what. My husband was a good person at heart but he chose a different path from the one I chose and the two were not cohesive. My absurd desire to be married and to finish having children by a certain age clouded my judgment. There was no way I should have gotten married prior to him at least starting school and working legitimately. There was no way I should have involved my son in that unstable situation much less to bring another child into it. Things could have gone in a completely different direction and I could have been the one behind bars and my children could have been growing up without either parent. Love is not the answer.

Chapter 6

THE WUSS

Please understand that this was devastating time for my kids and me. The arrest and subsequent deportation affected my job, my demeanor, my relationship with his family, my whole outlook. My family really didn't know what was going on so they were very disappointed when everything came to light. It was an ordeal from hell. He took all of his anger out on me and I allowed him to. I figured it was the least I could do since I was free and he was away from everything he knew. Eventually I decided to divorce him, which took almost a year. Though it was done mostly for legal reasons, he never forgave me. I had no intention of moving to Trinidad and the relationship was beyond repair. I thought my chances of being happy were over. Who wanted a divorced mother of two, with children from two different fathers?

A few months before I actually filed for divorce, my brother announced he was getting married. It was the summer of 2003. I really didn't know his fiancé very well but I decided to help with the wedding arrangements and was asked to be a bridesmaid. At the bridal shower, I laid eyes on the cutest guy I had seen in a long time. I couldn't even look at another guy since my husband had been arrested but this one stirred something inside me. I had a major crush on Tiger Woods and he looked so much like him. Great news, he was going to be in the wedding too. There was a lot of flirting going on between the shower, rehearsals and actual wedding. I had butterflies in my stomach whenever I saw him. What the hell was going on with me? I felt like a teenager again.

At the wedding, as he sang, I swore he was singing to me. Our faces must have given it away because everyone was looking at us instead of the bride and groom. Unfortunately, we weren't partnered up so we barely got to dance at the reception that night. After the ceremony we both went to the newlyweds' house to help them tidy up and prepare to leave for their honeymoon; that's where we exchanged numbers and had the first getting-to-know-you talk.

We had a couple of dates which were nothing short of magical and when we went to the post-wedding family dinner we actually fed each other. The newlyweds were sitting there confused thinking *shouldn't we be the ones doing that?* But that's how it was; the feelings were so sweet and so strong, so fast. Our first kiss, well to this day, it was the best ever. It took our breaths away and my heart literally skipped a beat.

He lived alone, didn't have any children, was apparently a momma's boy, about the same age as me and could cook his ass off. Tiger Woo as I called him also sang somewhat professionally and had an entire set-up in his home to record and produce songs. He talked about finishing the second bedroom as a recording booth but the supplies to finish the project lay on the floor. Being the control freak I am, I encouraged him to pursue his dream. Offered to help him finish the room and tried to get him to go back in the studio. I thought his songs were great, listened to his homemade CDs all the time and played them for anyone who'd listen. Isn't it amazing how love is blind and deaf? Deep down, his lack of motivation annoyed me though. It was a major problem for me. I couldn't understand why he wasn't pursuing something he so obviously loved. But despite that minor issue, I was again totally gone.

We didn't rush into sex, I can honestly say that we did everything the right way. We got to know each other; we took walks on the Promenade, went on picnics, sat and talked for hours. Talked about what we wanted out of life, what we wanted from each other and we were really open and honest. For some reason, I couldn't lie to him, couldn't hold anything back. I wanted him to know everything up front. When we did take it to the physical level it was so right, like a missing puzzle piece. Eventually he met my kids and they instantly took to him. My daughter was just about to turn 4 and my son just turned 12. All was so right. You couldn't tell me at that time that I hadn't found *The One.* So far, no red flags.

However, I was technically still married and this was a problem for him. We talked at length about my situation, I was honest with him but I had not yet taken that final step to file the papers. My husband, who was still in jail, knew I wanted to separate us legally but also knew that he would face deportation once he served his time. He didn't want me to divorce him just yet because he thought being married to an American citizen might prevent his deportation. That's why he has never forgiven me to this day. I was torn between what was best for me and what might help him.

Then it happened, quite suddenly and out of the blue. My Tiger Woo emailed me and said that he *"couldn't be a father to my children"* and therefore couldn't continue the relationship. It was the first time in my life that I was devastated by a man in that way. I cried like a baby. I emailed him back and confessed that I had fallen in love with him. My new sister-in-law said that telling him that was a huge mistake but it was how I felt at the time. I played every moment we spent together over and over in my head trying to figure out where I went wrong. Was I too clingy? Too mushy? Too aggressive? Not aggressive enough? It just didn't make sense. His birthday was approaching and I had already bought him a present so I asked if I could bring it over. His favorite drink was a dirty martini, the dirtier the better. I had bought him a set of martini glasses and a cocktail shaker which I had hoped we would have used together. When I stopped by to give him the gift, I was hoping for some insight into why he ended it. I assured him that I wasn't looking for a father for my kids, that I was looking for a partner but he didn't have much to say. It was a sad goodbye but I told myself that if he couldn't accept me and my children then he wasn't the right man for me.

Over the next few months as my sister-in-law tried and tried to fix things between us, I would come to find out that the real reason he broke up with me was because things were happening too fast and because I was still married. He couldn't handle the speed at which our feelings were developing especially since my life was so uncertain at that time.

I filed for divorce the following month.

What did I learn?

I am not sure I could have done anything different here except to have simply waited until I was completely divorced. But we met when we met. If anything, he could have been more honest about his apprehension and maybe we could have merely decided to take things much slower. This is one relationship that I think about a lot to this day. I have this feeling that his lack of motivation would have eventually gotten the best of me. He was content with not pursuing his dream, I wasn't. This was a clear case of not being able to make a person into someone they're not.

Chapter 7

THE JAMAICAN

My husband's arrest and my filing for divorce took a serious toll on me. Now add to that the recent quickie courtship and breakup . . . I was an emotional wreck. I was an assistant nurse manager of a highly stressful department and many times I had to retreat to my office in tears. I couldn't talk to many people at my job about my situation as it would have been unprofessional but there was one person that knew the whole story. He was the unit secretary who had helped me out as a friend over the years even when my husband was still around. He had changed my flat tire once and helped us move. He was the one who comforted me when I cried, when my ex-husband called and yelled at me or when I just needed a shoulder to cry on.

I never looked at him in any other way but as a friend; after all he was 9 years younger than me. I was his boss but one day he tried his luck and I was just vulnerable enough to fall for it. Now first you need to understand that when you looked at this man, he looked like a virgin. Almost like a nerd, one might even venture to think he was gay. So when he told me one day that he wanted to suck my breasts at work, I was totally thrown off. I laughed at this dude, literally. He went on to tell me that he'd fantasized about me for years and that he wanted a chance to make me feel good since I was going through so much.
"What can you do?" I asked.
"Let me show you," he suggested.
I decided right then that it was time for me to change things up. No more relationships, no more trying to find Mr. Right, no more fantasizing, no more looking for *The One*. From now on, I was going to be just like a man. No strings attached, just sex, have fun, keep it moving. I would give

the young boy a chance, he was so eager to please. I couldn't disappoint him.

I let him come over to my house. We drank and tried to find a way past the awkwardness. The angel on my shoulder was screaming to stop. This was not me, felt wrong. The devil on my other shoulder was whispering for me to get laid, forget about the rest and just enjoy the moment. I grabbed his dick, sized it up. It was a bit smaller than I was used to. That made me want to stop, there was nothing more annoying than an average-sized dick. I tried to back out but he was begging, pleading, telling me how long he's wanted me. It felt good to hear after so much rejection. I let him fuck me; it was okay, just okay. But it did the job.

Somehow he stuck around for the next three years. My Jamaican stood by me through a major surgery, my divorce, the resulting bacchanal, the family drama, all of it. He treated me like a queen and made life easier for me. He cooked, cleaned, did anything I asked. The sex vastly improved, all he needed was a little coaching. But I knew in my heart it couldn't go anywhere. I was in my early thirties and he was in his early twenties, I had two children by two different men and had no intention of having any more. He insisted that he didn't want kids that mine were enough but I knew better; knew that one day he would regret staying with someone like me. In addition, after about 2 years of being together he started developing a jealous streak and drinking a bit more than usual. Those two factors began to drive a wedge between us. We started arguing a lot and every time we broke up I breathed a sigh of relief but he begged back and I gave in every time.

My goody goody was turning into a bad boy. It was almost as if he was trying so hard to be more Jamaican if you get where I'm coming from. Like he needed to prove something, it was so not him, not the person I knew. One night, we were driving home on the Interboro Parkway which is an infamous road that runs from Brooklyn to Queens; the kids were in the car. Now my Jamaican was very much into cars and driving, considered himself an excellent driver and viewed it more as a sport. Someone had cut him off on the road and he proceeded to pursue this guy at a very high speed on this very narrow two lane road which was bordered by a forest and a concrete divider. I screamed for him to stop, reminding him that the kids were in the car but he continued until he ran the other car into the divider. When he was done, I was so angry and surprised that he would do something so stupid that put the children in danger. Red Flag! This was the turning point, this was the perfect opportunity to end it but I didn't. He begged, I bowed.

Jealousy was and is a major turn off for me as I am the total opposite. Now don't get me wrong, if it's thrown in my face of course I'm going to react it but I am not the type to snoop. Not the type to look into a phonebook, go through my guy's pockets or get vex if he talks or dances with someone else. I try to behave as I would want him to behave and if it's good for me then I figure it should be good for him. Culturally, we were different. I had dated Jamaican men before and my experience with them was that they're somewhat possessive as opposed to Trinidadian men who are a bit more comfortable with their women dancing with other guys. It was very hard for him to grasp this concept at first. He just didn't get it and the longer we were together the more it bothered him. If we went to a party together, he got upset if I said hello to too many guys but these were people I knew before him. It was the topic of many a discussion.

In the last year of our relationship, the Jamaican started car shopping. He saved about $6,000 and he was looking for a very particular car, a black on black Maxima. We searched lot after lot and had yet to find one but we did stumble across a black on black Infiniti QX4. Of course it was way over his budget, priced at about $12,000. He fell in love with it, tried to finance the balance but he had bad credit and the payments were working out to be too high. So what did my dumb ass do? I offered to put the balance on my credit card and he promised to pay me back in lump sums. I think I did it because I felt like he had done so much for me and I wanted to do something for him. However things started to go sour and he crashed the car. It wasn't totaled but it was never the same so he sold it, got another vehicle but still hadn't paid me back in full.

In the winter of 2006, after too many breakups, I gave up. It was just too hard, my heart wasn't into and I don't think his was either. I think he finally grew up and realized we grew apart. When we finally parted ways for the last time, he stilled owed me about $4,000. He was only paying the minimum each month.

What did I learn?

Age may just be a number but where we are in life matters and sometimes age does matter. 10 years difference is significant especially when one person is just starting out in life and the other has been through hell and back. Though this relationship was vital at that time in my life and brought me back from the deepest lows, I made a crucial mistake in judgment. Do not ever take out a line of credit for a man, register a car in their name, put something expensive on your credit card or lend them a significant amount of money unless you are married to them. The amount differs from person to person and doesn't really matter but the rule applies. It's the same rule as friends lending friends money; unless you can afford for them to not pay you back, it's a bad idea.

Chapter 8

DADDY OF THE YEAR

Now though we are exploring my past relationships, my ex-boyfriends, there is one relationship that has to be discussed though he was never really my boyfriend. At least not for more than a week.

2007 was fast approaching and as usual my friends and I were preparing for Trinidad carnival which was in February of 2007. Anyone who has ever gone on a vacation with a large group of people knows that it takes months of preparation; at least it does if you want to do the damn thing right. Emails were a plenty, back and forth between the group, about 80 a day discussing everything from our costumes, to accommodations, to which parties we were attending. I didn't even get to read half of the emails so I missed many of the discussions; not realizing that a new guy had been added to our group. Apparently there was much conversation about him being excited to see me again. Again?

Rewind about 7 years, Labor Day in Brooklyn. My brother and I usually went to the parade together; this year his friend joined us. It was a miserable rainy day but I'll never forget what he had on; work boots, cut-off jean shorts and a hoodie which was pulled low over his head. All I could see were dimples and I couldn't wait to dance with him. He had that bad boy look that caught my attention. Unfortunately, we got separated by the crowd before I could get my hands on him and I never saw him again. According to my brother and his wife, he'd been asking about me since then but my brother never told me or relayed any of the messages he sent.

February 2007 arrived and we were off to Trinidad. I was secretly dying to see him again but I played it very cool. Finally I saw him and there were those dimples again, I was instantly weak. For the next week we were flirted with each other, partied and had so much fun together but also within the group. Most of us flew home on the same flight, we ended up sitting together. He got sick on the trip with a fever and throat infection so we cuddled under the blankets and I played nurse. It was like it we already knew each other, no awkwardness, no stressful first date; it was all very natural.

Until we landed; then his demeanor changed completely. He was being picked up by his daughter's mother but I didn't know exactly what the situation between them was. He called me when he got home and there was this awkwardness that wasn't there before. I thought maybe he had a girlfriend and just kind of realized that the vacation was over and now it was back to reality but he denied having one.

We went out on a few dates, he didn't exactly wine and dine me but we enjoyed each other's company as much as his schedule would allow. Our daughters were two years apart so we had something in common. The problem was though he had a good job, he was required to get up at 4:30 in the morning so he was always tired. He had custody of his daughter every other weekend and on those weekends, he didn't see me. He was a really good father, totally focused on his daughter but after a while, even on his free weekends something always came up. He didn't really drink alcohol much, didn't really like to party much and kind of just wanted to stay home which was okay with me, to a point. He thought I went out too much and wanted to know when I would slow down. To me, since he met me like this, he should accept me like this so love me or leave me. It got to a point where I would feel funny even if I had a drink in front of him.

The thing was the sex was amazing and I couldn't get enough of him; I would fiend for this man. Even if three weeks went by, when he texted me, my pussy jumped, literally. There was something about him that intimidated me though, I never felt quite able to express myself, to relax around him. Maybe because I knew he disapproved of my lifestyle which was by no means crazy, I just liked to party. But he was so critical of it and of me. By Thursday of each week I was already planning what we'd do for the weekend. I'd gingerly ask him what his plans were hoping that they included me. If it didn't, I'd suggest going out to dinner or something similar and sometimes he'd say, "I'm not taking my daughter to a babysitter so we can go out. She didn't ask to be here, I brought her into this world."

Huh?

I'd say, "We need adult time. Everything is a balance. How are you going to be happy if you never have fun with people your own age? With me?"

But he didn't agree. To him, being home with his daughter was enough, at least that's what he said. He wouldn't even let his mother watch the child for a few hours so that we could do something together. The way I saw it, the weekend he didn't have his daughter should have been my weekend but he didn't see it that way. I spent many nights there especially when I had to work the weekend but I always left early in the morning, before he got up. I figured if he wanted me to stay, he would have asked.

One day as I was braiding his hair, a particularly good day, I asked him if I was his girlfriend. Now I know we never had the talk about commitment but I wanted to see what he'd say and we were already having some conversation about relationships or something.
He said, "Let's not label it; it's going just fine the way it is." Wow, why did that hurt so much? I realized then that he wasn't mine and probably never would be.

We continued more on than off for the next few of years. At times, I would stop seeing him because I felt that he would never give me what I wanted but then I would get that text and boom! "Can I come and eat you?" It was just that easy. I would date other people during our times apart but I'd always compare them to him and since I hadn't met anyone special, I would end up back in his arms.

Then in the summer of 2009, during one of our hiatuses, he called. Immediately my body and heart responded; this is how it was between us. I'd walk away because he'd never say or do the right thing and then a call or text from him sent me into a whirlwind. This time I was at a party, in the rain, having a great time. I tried to get him to come and meet me there. He said he was in the middle of getting a tattoo. That confused me because even though he had a couple already, he had never expressed a desire to get another.

He never met me that day but he did come by my job a few days later. I asked to see the tattoo but he was very reluctant. He finally showed me, it was on his upper arm but he was covering the bottom part of it with his hand. The part that I could see was of a male lion with what looked to me like a female and an even smaller lion. I asked him if he got married thinking the female lion was the wife and the smaller one, his daughter. He denied it. I had to see the rest of it and after much pulling and tugging, the rest of the tattoo was revealed. It had two names at the bottom; one was his daughter's and the other was a boy's name. What the fuck? I asked him if he had a baby, he denied that also. I was very confused. He said he put the boy's name because that was the name that he wanted for his next child.

So you want me to believe that you tattooed the name of a child that hasn't even been conceived yet?

I was done; I jumped out of the car, tired of his fucking games. Later that night he called me, we talked and he admitted that he indeed had a baby. A boy, nine months old now but he would not reveal who the mother was. Then he had the nerve to ask me if I would stand by him. You see something like this had happened to him before. He was dating a woman with whom he was very interested in but casually slept with another and she ended up pregnant. The woman who got pregnant was someone who he slept with occasionally; she, according to him, had a plan. He claimed that he was asleep when the woman raped him then disappeared for months. When she resurfaced, she informed him that she was pregnant; he was now living with the first woman. He didn't believe her so they had the paternity testing done after the child was born. The woman he was living with stood by him through the entire ordeal and they remained together until a year or so before he and I met. Now he expected me to do the same.

Stand by what? Wasn't I the same person who wasn't good enough to be your girlfriend?

I felt totally heartbroken and confused. I really thought that somehow, someway, despite the back and forth, the on and off, that we'd eventually get it together. I always thought we'd end up together. This was way too much for me to handle. I was laying on the bed with the phone to my ear as the tears streamed down my face listening to his story.

He came by the next day. I sat in his jeep waiting to hear what he had to say. Maybe there was something he could say that would make this situation make sense. It was raining and I sat listening to him explain why he hadn't told me before.
"I knew you'd get mad. I just couldn't find the words to tell you," he said.
"How he could let this happen?" I asked. He didn't have an answer. But honestly, I had neither a commitment to this man nor he to me. We weren't a couple, weren't even together when the woman got pregnant. Why was I mad? Did I have the right to be? Could I stay in this dysfunctional so-called relationship? Could I deal with this?

He had no magic words, no apologies or promises; nothing but excuses. He wouldn't even tell me who the mother of the baby was or how he allowed himself, a seemingly intelligent man, to get caught, again. He actually had more of an attitude than I did.

Lightning does not strike twice in the same place.

I sat waiting for the rain to stop, wishing for it to stop so I could escape. I had never felt so betrayed; I was hurting because I couldn't get past the unnecessary lying about the child and the tattoo. I finally jumped out of his car and vowed to let him go, for good.

What did I learn?

This is a tough one because we never had a commitment therefore technically; I can't say he cheated on me or disrespected me. We weren't speaking when he impregnated the woman who had his son. However, my dear friend Maria, the hater, pointed something out to me. Whenever I expressed my love for him, she would ask me "What did he ever do to deserve your love?" I honestly couldn't think of one thing. Besides picking me up from the hospital after one of my surgeries; no other random acts of kindness, no concern for how I paid my bills or whether I had enough food to feed the children, no coming over on Sundays to wash my car or anything of the sort. He was good on paper, we were the same age, knew a lot of the same people hence compatible. She insisted that I wasn't in love but in love with the idea of being in love. Aha! Light bulbs started flashing in my head. I heard what she said, believed it, it made sense to me but could I put into practice? I had to stop feeling like a victim, like men were treating me poorly. No, people can only treat you how you allow them to and I had to learn to command better. To believe that I deserved better and right then, I didn't.

Chapter 9

BUBBALICIOUS

I spent the next 6 months dating casually with a couple of different guys, enjoying being wined and dined. Nice restaurants, going to interesting spots I'd never been to, being cooked for. I had no desire to settle down or start a relationship. I was having fun, being flirtatious and trying my best to keep my mind off of him. I wanted to hate him, wanted to forget him but I knew he'd always be there lingering in the back of my mind. However, I would never call him nor did he reach out to me.

Boxing Day 2009; we were at a party and this very pushy guy who I had never seen before was hanging out with a friend of ours, buying us drinks. I didn't really focus on him or how he looked but I gave him a few courtesy dances. At the end of the party which was 6 in the morning, we ventured outside to buy soup from a vendor on the street. The guy was still hanging around, begging for my number which I had no desire or intention of giving. Our mutual friend was also pleading that I give him a chance. I still hadn't taken a proper look but I gave him my number anyway. I wasn't even thinking that he would call and my new take on meeting men was to keep it light and flirty but he did call; about an hour later and every morning and evening, everyday thereafter. He was a persistent mother-fucker. He wanted to take me to dinner, to come visit but I truly wasn't interested. I must admit, though I'm not a phone person, the conversations always flowed. He rarely texted me, which was and still is a major turn-off as most guys only text, he always picked up the phone and called.

Maria was having a birthday party two weeks later just after New Year's, I invited Bubbalicious. I was cordial but didn't want to send mixed signals so I treated him like any other guest. Before the night was over an argument broke out. My other dear friend, Wendy, was arguing with another girl; it somehow escalated and the men became involved. We were freaking out because we just found out that very night that Wendy was pregnant so Maria and I intervened to stop the argument. Out of nowhere Bubba jumped in, pushed me out of the way and broke up everything. The party was over. Why would he do that? He didn't even know us and he got involved like that? He's trying way too hard.

We continued talking several times a day over the next few weeks. I mentioned during one of our talks that I was taking my car in for brakes and Bubba was very concerned about how I would get to work and how I would pick my daughter up from school. The next thing I knew, he was outside my apartment insisting that we switch cars for the night. He wanted to take my car to his mechanic and he wanted me to take his Range Rover.

This guy was nuts.

Every bone in my body was screaming No! But I convinced myself that I deserved to be treated nicely for a change since no one had ever offered to do things like that for me before and quite frankly, it felt nice. He brought my car back the next day with new brakes, sparkling clean. I still wasn't interested though, there was no sexual spark. He continued with the royal treatment though; dinner at a very fancy restaurant in Hastings-on-the-Hudson, he dropped my son to Prep school which was over 100 miles away in New Jersey, he paid for my shopping at Target and sent the first of many deliveries of roses to my job. He was unrelenting but I liked his style. At least he knew how to court a woman but I still wasn't the least bit attracted to him, at least not physically. He did have a way about him though, he was charismatic and that was attractive. He knew how to take care of things, of everything. He made me feel that he would be there to solve all my problems, not matter how big or small. He made me feel safe. He told me in no uncertain terms that I would fall in love with him and that the next man I dated would have a hard act to follow since he had planned on spoiling me.

Rolling my eyes, I just couldn't see it.

He also had connections or so he claimed. He worked for the city, some high level job that gave him certain security clearances. He knew so many people in so many different places. We'd go to dinner at what I thought was a random restaurant; he knew the owner, the doorman and the bartender. He'd get pulled over for not wearing a seatbelt, which he never did; he'd mention a few names and walk away free. Also, he was a talker. He'd enter a room and command it with his presence. Bubba was here! Within minutes he'd be talking to just about everyone. That's how he was. It was an attractive quality at the time. But he was also a know-it-all who would argue with anyone about anything and felt no shame in telling a lawyer that he didn't know how to try a case. He had a tendency of putting his finger in people's face when making a point; it was very embarrassing and despite me pointing this out to him, he saw nothing wrong with it. I actually think it was a tactic to intimidate people.

Then he dropped the bomb; he was married. Separated but still married as far as I was concerned. According to him, he left his wife a few weeks ago after months of them sleeping apart. He stated that they lived in a huge house in New Jersey and he had left most of his belongings behind. He was now living with a cousin in Brooklyn, temporarily. Now of course, this is where it should have ended. No need for further explanation, he was married. Red Flag! Red Flag! He tried to convince me that he was 100% sure that he wasn't going back, that his wife of 15 years had done such unforgiveable things to him that he could never go back to her. I should have just stopped right here. But I told myself that since I wasn't really attracted to him, there's no harm. I'd just play along and enjoy the ride.

Over the next few weeks we continued getting to know each other. He kept with the flowers, great restaurants and just generally making sure I wanted for nothing. One day we passed by another one of his cousin's house to check on his dog and ended up hanging out for a while having drinks and watching TV. Bubba made his move; he wanted to fuck me right on the couch. I felt the bulge in his pants and couldn't help but smile.
"You hit the jackpot nigga!" he yelled with a big grin on his face. Really? I couldn't believe he was using that word. But I still wasn't ready yet. It would take me another few weeks and though he was huge, he was not exactly skilled in the art of love-making. It's so true; a big dick does not a good lover make. This one would need some work, lots.

Trinidad carnival followed in February and we had a fantastic time. I split my time between Bubba and Maria and by the end of the trip; somehow we ended up a couple. He made me feel beautiful and I managed to look past the physical and just enjoyed the person that he was. My friends were wondering what the hell was wrong with me, they couldn't understand what I saw in him. He was tall with a medium build but he had a huge baller-belly, as he called it and though he had great skin, he was not particularly handsome. It was a face you either loved or hated and though I didn't love it, I loved the way he treated me. They nicknamed him Bubbalicious.

Looks are not everything.

I was happy as a lamb though, until a few months later. Talk of the divorce was minimal as he claimed to be in the process of hiding assets from his wife's lawyer. It would take a bit longer than usual as he had several companies, properties and accounts that had to be hidden. Bubba alluded to being a millionaire but never really confirmed just how much of a millionaire he was.

May 2010; Maria, Wendy and I were throwing a party. A few years ago we formed a group that gave parties, fund raisers and family events. I explained this very clearly to Bubba when we first met. I told him that I was involved in a group and that my involvement required me to attend lots of functions and it was important for me to be friendly. That friendliness would also be extended to men but that these were men who were potential customers. I explained to him that jealousy would not be tolerated because I was not a jealous person and didn't expect him to be. He said he understood and was glad because he too knew lots of people.

The party was in full swing and I was making my rounds since Wendy was pregnant and pretty much sitting, handling the bar transactions; Maria arrived late. After dancing with a very good friend of mine I went to check on Bubba who was visibly pissed. He started yelling and screaming at me in the party; everyone could see. He very dramatically handed me my house key and stormed out, I was so embarrassed so I followed him outside. Apparently, while I was dancing with my friend, Maria went to talk to Bubba and his cousin. He told me that she stood in front of him and tried to block him from seeing me dancing; he insisted that Maria was blocking him from seeing because she knew that there was something going on between the guy and me.

What? You've got to be kidding.

We continued arguing outside but there was no convincing him so I stopped talking. I just let him go on and on and the more I saw his contorted face screaming at me, the clearer things became. I began to see his ugliness. Flag on the play! Now see, this would have been the perfect time for me to have walked away and not look back. Jealousy would not be tolerated I said but I did not hold true to my own standards. We eventually made up after a few dozen roses and promises of this type of thing never happening again but it left me skeptical and conscious of my movements when we went out. Should I stand next to him all night? Could I talk to any guys that I knew without it causing a fight? I was on pins and needles.

The relationship continued but new concerns arose. Bubba didn't have children and I broke my own rule about dating men without children. And wouldn't you know it, my kids hated him. Of course this was a deal breaker but being the person that I am, I first tried everything to work it out. I talked to Bubba, tried to get him to see what he apparently couldn't but it never quite worked. So I kept them apart as much as possible even though I knew deep down there was no future for us. But I also didn't feel like the greatest mother in the world and I wanted to be fair and really make sure there wasn't something that I wasn't noticing, in me; in my way of mothering. Everyone always thought I spoiled them. He told me that my son needed a man to raise him and my daughter was manipulative and no man would be good enough for me. He felt that was why she didn't like him. Why was I allowing him to get in my head like that?

Who are you to analyze or criticize my children or my method of parenting especially when you don't have any of your own?

He was trying hard to convince me that his presence in our life was detrimental to my children's very survival. He was playing my single mother card making me feel guilty that my children were lacking something and it was working. My son was away at college so he didn't have to see or deal with Bubba but my daughter did. I talked to him, Bubba, time and time again about the way he spoke to my daughter thinking he may not be aware of the tone of his voice or the way he looked at her but he refused to acknowledge it. I finally asked him not to get involved when it came to her, to leave that to me. He agreed but it didn't last too long, his overbearing personality wouldn't allow him to stay quiet. It was a never-ending battle between us.

November 2010; we were at a Mexican restaurant celebrating my birthday having margaritas and fried ice cream when I received a call from Daddy of the Year. I had removed his name from my phone but I knew his number right away. I answered, not wanting to raise suspicion by not answering and we talked briefly. He called to wish me a happy birthday and said that he missed me. My heart leapt but I played it cool and went back to my margarita and ice cream. Of course I got drilled as to who called and I knew that he saw the number when the phone rang so I told him who it was. I saw no reason to lie and I wasn't very good at it anyway. Thankfully he didn't make an issue of it. That was the first time I had heard from Daddy him since last year; my head was spinning but I continued playing it cool.

The following month, I found out that I needed a breast biopsy and the possibility of me having breast cancer temporarily brought us close again. The thought of me having cancer was just too much to bear for him since his wife had it a few years prior and had thankfully overcome it. I ended up having to undergo minor breast surgery to remove the mass and had to wait a week for the pathology results. Bubba was there supporting me through the whole ordeal. He was great and I forgot about all the negatives and tried to focus on the positives. I thought maybe the scare would calm him down. The pathology report was negative, I was safe for now. Maybe there was hope for us.

I tried to make Christmas extra special hoping that it would bring us together as a family but that band aid soon fell off; it just didn't work. The children were not feeling it and our family time was awkward and forced. Soon the sex, which was never that great, became downright unbearable. As a matter of fact, it got to a point where I could barely stand him touching me; he began to notice the change and asked me if he turned me off. What was I supposed to say, yes? Even I wasn't that mean. I played it off but I knew and he knew what was up; things were going downhill. From the beginning of the relationship Bubba had suggested that I purchase a foreclosure to get out of debt and amass some money; this was something he had been doing for years on the side and said that's how he made his real money. Every so often I would ask him if he found a suitable property for me but he always came up empty. Now it was a year since we met and I was starting to feel as if he was either lying about finding a house for me or using it as a way to hold on to me. I was most definitely putting extra effort into us because I desperately needed the money. I was willing to hang on to him figuring if he didn't find a property for me, I could benefit in some other way. Maybe I'd meet one of his friends with connections and make a business contact. I had to be smarter; it was time to think with my head and not my heart.

2011 arrived, Trinidad carnival was coming up again and I wanted to go. All my friends were going but I had no one to take care of my daughter; her winter recess didn't coincide with the week I needed to go, so I couldn't even take her with me. Bubba went though, for the first time, with his friends. While he was there he called me every few hours giving me the blow-by-blow details of all the craziness that was going on and of course this was just making me want to go even more. He claimed that he was in his room most of the time whilst everyone else was hanging out by the pool, looking for a last minute ticket for me. He wanted me to come down just for the weekend and leave my daughter with my mom. I looked for a seat on the only airline that had direct flights as did he but everything was sold out, even first class which he said he'd pay for. Something about the way he was saying it though made me envision him boasting to everyone that he was trying to bring me down first class just for a couple of days; he had that immodest way about him. I could see him bragging poolside at the Hyatt holding court for anyone who'd listen.

That was his way and it was becoming more and more apparent as the time went by. Character traits that in the beginning were attractive had changed into something ugly. Protective became jealous. Strong became over-bearing. Confident became arrogant. Initially my family liked him but now even they were no longer fans and were beginning to notice the way that he looked at my daughter; like she irritated him. When confronted about it, he said he was brought up to believe that children were meant to be seen and not heard. He found her to be too much and thought that my bedroom door should stay closed with her in her room at all times. He couldn't understand why I didn't have a lock on my door; so he put one on. I told him I wasn't raised to lock my door and there was no way I would expect my 10 year old daughter to stay in her room all the time. I raised my children to feel free to express themselves; we were constantly arguing over things like this.

Shortly after he returned from carnival I received a text from Daddy of the Year. It said that he loved me and wanted us to be together, asked if I was seeing anyone. I replied that I had someone but wasn't too happy. I was heading down a dangerous path, I knew it, but I guess I was looking for a savior. I felt like I couldn't get away from this man, Bubba, on my own. At the same time, I couldn't believe the expression of love from Daddy, love? He never used that word before. Why now? Because I was with someone else? That initial text started a series of conversations between us and very soon I was hiding my phone whenever Bubba came over.

Eventually I got busted. A text came through when Bubba was sitting next to me; he recognized the number immediately and demanded to know what it said. This started a huge fight because there was no way I could show him. He tried to wring the phone out of my hand while I tried to erase the text. He demanded to know how long I'd been communicating with him and said he would get a printout of my phone calls and texts so I had better not lie. He had hook ups everywhere; banks, phone companies, police, the list went on and I knew he could get it. I was panicked of course but I stood my ground. Invasion of privacy! He didn't care. I stood there and read the text to him leaving out the juice parts. He was so angry and I started to panic. Bubba threatened to call him, Daddy, to ask him just why he was texting me! Oh Lord, this couldn't end well. I begged him not to and promised to end all contact.

The next night Bubba brought a printout of all the texts and phone calls between Daddy and me; there was dozens. I didn't even realize there were that many. He was furious; thank God my daughter wasn't home. He went into my dirty laundry and pulled out my panties to examine them. He accused me of having sex with Daddy and said my panties would prove it. Now I was really scared though I hadn't done anything wrong. Okay, the texting was wrong but he was acting irrationally. I tried not to argue back because we were home alone. He was shouting and screaming so I ran into the bathroom to lock myself in but he was fast, so fast. He barricaded me in the bathroom and continued to scream at me, accusing me of all kinds of things. He grabbed me by the back of my neck and dragged me into the bedroom. Still holding my neck, he threw me onto the bed. He then hit me with one of my stuffed animals; it didn't hurt but all I could think was that he'd rather hit me with something else. I start crying and he yelled at me to stop with the crocodile tears. I stayed quiet, too afraid to yell back. He looked around and started picking up all the gifts that he gave me over the last year. The quilt and sheets off of the bed, the Gucci bag he bought me for Christmas, the iPad he bought for my birthday, the slippers he bought me at the beach when mine got washed away by the tide. He gathered all of them and stuffed them in a garbage bag all the while yelling that I didn't deserve anything. He said that he treated me so good and I was so bad to him. He went into the kitchen and poured out all of the alcohol; he bought it so it had to go.

"I need a truck to back up in here and get all the shit I bought for you out!" he yelled.

Take it! Take all of it! Reproachful fuck!

I ran back into my bedroom to get away from the madman, locked my door with the lock he put on and prayed that he would leave. He broke down the door. He said he put on the lock so it too had to go.

Oh I'm fucked now.

As he barreled into the room, I just sat there. Sat there and waited for the bullet or the knife or the blow that would kill me. I pictured the headline in tomorrow's paper. *Mother of Two Found Dead!* How many times had I read a similar headline and wondered what kind of people did that happen to; low class surely. And here I was facing death or a good beating and all I could do was wait for it and blame myself.

You really did it now.

He asks why I'm just sitting there. "Aren't you going to say anything?" he yells.
"Are you gonna kill me?" I ask softly.
"Kill you? Kill you? I wouldn't waste a bullet on your ass", he snorts.
With that he left. Left with my sheets and quilt, iPad, Gucci bag and slippers but I was unharmed; at least physically. I cried and cried but I was more afraid he'd return as he had keys. I called Maria, told her what took place and she was ready to drive to my house.
"Change the locks, now!" she said.
"Tomorrow, it's too late now", I answered.
Maria was afraid for me but I told her that I would be okay. If I needed her, I would call her.

Then Daddy called. He heard the distress in my voice and said he was coming over. I briefly gave him the rundown of the argument and Bubba's abrupt departure.
"What if he's waiting outside and sees you," I said.
We agreed that I would come downstairs to talk. When he pulled up I slowly made my way to the car, looking around for any sign of Bubba. I got into his car and told him to drive away so we could park and talk. Daddy told me that he loved me and was ready for us to be together. A real couple. We both agreed that this was the worst possible time

to start a relationship but we did agree to take it extremely slow. Nothing physical for now, just slowly get to know each other again. I was elated as I had been waiting to hear for this for 4 years.

Before we go any further though, I'm going to need you to answer some questions.

I asked him about the mother of his son, I needed to know who she was. He hesitated.

Oh my Lord. Don't tell me it's the same woman who you have your daughter with?

"Yes", he admitted. But assured me that they were not together and he had never loved her. I want to believe him so badly.

Can I deal with this? This was just too much.

Then he told me something that shook me to the core. He told me that the mother of his children actually lived with him. "Well she doesn't really live there, she's just there to help with the kids," he explained.

What?

He told me in his most sincere voice that he grew up without both his parents and he wanted very much for his children to live with him but his crazy work schedule made that difficult. He didn't get home until 11:30 at night and he'd rather have their mother take care of the children than a complete stranger.

Where does she sleep?

He said she slept in their daughter's room. That they barely spoke, didn't really get along well but he had to make this sacrifice for his children. He said he made his bed and now he must sleep in it and wouldn't blame me if I walked away knowing the situation.

Hearing this new revelation was heart-wrenching but I took a leap of faith and decided to believe everything he said, at least for now. I wanted this to work so I was willing to take that leap; after all, I had waited years for this. I asked one last question, one that he didn't answer right away so I told him to think about it.

How are you going to fit me into your life?

I went back upstairs, put the chain on my door, thought about all the craziness of the last year with Bubba and dreamt about a future with Daddy.

A few weeks weeks later after ignoring his way too many calls and text messages; I got an unexpected call at work from Bubba. He called to apologize for sticking me with the cable bill. You see, without my permission, he hooked up a new cable in my apartment which was supposed to save me money; one of his hook-ups that didn't work out. I ended up having to pay $700; he kept promising to pay me back but then we broke up. He admitted that he purposely didn't pay the bill because he was mad at me and now wanted to give me back the money. He also wanted to know if I still had the few bits and pieces he'd left behind.

Of course I do; if you think I would throw them out, you really never knew me.

He asked if he could come by to drop the money and pick his stuff up. I told him it was a bad idea especially since my daughter was home and should not see him so we arranged to meet in the lobby. He also wanted to let me know that his divorce was final, that he was moving back into his house which he was renovating from top to bottom and that he just ordered a convertible Bentley.

Whatever.

I met him in the lobby downstairs, I handed him the bag with his belongings and he turned to leave. I stood there dumbfounded.
"Where's my money?" I asked.
"Are you serious?" he replies so very dramatically, standing there looking totally confused.
I then realized that all he wanted was his things and he never had any intention of paying me back. No problem, the way I had to look at it was that I paid $700 to get this asshole out of my life. It was a bargain. I slowly turned and walked back upstairs leaving him standing there.

Have a good life, nigga.

What did I learn?

This was a tough one because even though he was married/ separated, that was not the cause of the demise of the relationship. I truly believed he was pursuing the divorce otherwise I would not have dated him. Something went wrong somewhere and I can only say that we were simply different people. We had different outlooks, viewpoints and opinions on important enough topics that made us incompatible such as child-rearing. There was no way we would have made it as a couple and there was nothing either of us could do about it.

Chapter 10

DADDY OF THE YEAR, TAKE 2

So we were officially a couple, it felt so weird. We really didn't get to see much of each other due to our conflicting work schedules but since we decided to take it slow, I was okay with it. One Saturday he came to pick me up to visit Wendy who had just been diagnosed with breast cancer. She was one of my dearest friends but also his. My phone was assaulted by texts from Bubba, last count was 40; I didn't bother to read them. As we drove, my attention focused on the pictures of his children that were hanging from the rear view mirror. I had already met his daughter many times but never his son. Now remember, this was the son that he had during one of our times apart. The one that he didn't tell me existed until he was 9 months old and only after I exposed his tattoo. His son's picture spun around as the car was moving and I couldn't stop staring at it. My eyes watered but I hid them.

He has a son.

The reality hit me and I felt sick to my stomach. Not toward the baby but toward the situation. He had two children for this woman, what did he want with me? Why didn't he try to work things out with her? I started to feel confused again. Meanwhile, Bubba kept calling and texting so I turned off my phone. The pictures bounced up and down, back and forth as we drove through Brooklyn. 2 years old, he's 2 years old, I thought. My daughter was 11; did I really want to go back to the baby stage? If I was going to be with this man, really be with this man then that meant his children would have to be in my life. I started to panic but I pushed the feeling away.

Daddy and I decided to start dating to get to know each other all over again. We both agreed that we never really had a chance to just spend time together or to talk about our goals and dreams. Small problem, he was now working the swing shift from 3:00 pm to 11:00 pm, the only time he had for me was 11:30 at night and sometimes he'd work 6 evenings per week. He could stop by on his way home but he was usually tired as was I by that time of the night. On his one day off, of course he needed to spend time with his children and just rest from the hectic work week. It was not an easy situation and I began to wonder where and if I could fit into his life. He easily fit into mine as my children had gotten to know him over the years but we were now in a relationship, things couldn't stay the same. At the end of the day, the whole point of being in a relationship is to build and to see where things might go. I just couldn't see where I and mine fit in.

We texted each other a couple of times a day and we talked on the phone every other. Days had passed and I hadn't seen him. I tried to stay up late in case he texted me that he was coming by after work but almost a week went by and I was getting frustrated. A second week was coming to an end so I asked if he'd like to go for drinks on Friday after work, he said Saturday would be better so we made a date.

Saturday finally came, he picked me up but he was cranky. He said he was tired from a long day at work. I suggested that we leave it for another day but he insisted. I was hesitant as I knew that his mood was not right especially since we hadn't seen each other for some time.

We headed to dinner but frankly, I regretted going. On the ride home, I asked him about the living situation with his children's mother. I really picked a bad time to do that.

Does she cook? Do you guys have dinner together? Who cleans the house?

Daddy got visibly irritated; he obviously did not like the questions. I wondered how I could put myself in this crazy situation if he refused to answer a few questions to put my mind at ease. Immediately my radar went off, something was not right. He wouldn't tell me her name, wouldn't discuss their arrangement and made it seem like he had no idea what went on in his own home. He said that he tried to not be home as much as possible but how could that be when staying away from her meant staying away from the children as well? I turned to him and asked one more question.

"Will I be able to come to your house when she's there?" I asked.
"No, she will get upset and tell my kids a bunch of shit," he answered. I was floored but I decided I would not end the night in an argument.
"I hope you are not lying to me," I finally said.

With that, I got out of the car and went upstairs. To me, the fact that he told me that I wouldn't be able to visit him at his house was unacceptable. If he and the woman decided to co-parent under one roof and if he was being truthful that there was nothing else to their relationship then why would she be upset if he had a girlfriend? Even if the woman had residual feelings, it was up to him to put her in check. It was up to him to make her understand that their arrangement was for thc benefit of the children and it was his house. The fact that he was allowing or anticipating a reaction told me that something was awry. Red Flag!

Another week went by and hadn't seen him. I talked to my friends, my aunt and my mother about the situation; they're all convinced that he was lying, that he and the girl were really together and he was trying to have his cake and eat it too. I felt like screaming. I didn't understand why he would go through all this trouble; he already had me exactly where he wanted me. Why didn't he just leave things the way they were? I spent the next few days contemplating their advice, going over all that I had heard in the last few weeks. I read back through my journals, read the entries about him over the years and I saw that time and time again I had written about feeling left out of his life, like an outsider. I realized that he had never gone out of his way to make me feel special or loved or included. It had always been words without action and I still felt like an outsider. Sadly, I had to face the fact that he was probably lying and that even if he wasn't lying, after all this time I shouldn't still feel like an afterthought. I had to demand better for myself. I had to expect better, to believe that I deserved better. When would I get this through my head?

Suddenly, a feeling of relief washed over me. Whatever spell had me tied to this man for so long had finally been broken and for the first time in 5 years, there was no feeling of longing, no feeling of anticipation, just a feeling of freedom.

I ended our relationship the next day.

What did learn?

Looking back, apparently nothing.

Chapter 11

THE END OR IS IT THE BEGINNING?

I wish life was like a DVR because there are several episodes I'd love to delete. If I had it my way, I would have married my high school sweetheart (I didn't have one, I'm just saying) and we would be living in our 4 bedroom house with a 2 car garage and our 2 perfect children would be on the honor roll in school. We'd have a retirement property in Trinidad, a summer house in Montauk, a time share in Hawaii and mind-blowing sex 4 times a week. Sounds great doesn't it? Funny though, I know not one couple that comes even close to that description so it really is a fantasy. But here I am, 42 and still trying. I don't know why I'm still trying because the fantasy never materialized therefore anything I achieve now would be second best, a consolation prize. Even if I find Mr. Right tomorrow, I haven't lived the life I wanted to. But maybe, just maybe, one day I'll get it right and it will be enough. If not then so be it. I've lived, I've loved and I have stories to tell.

So what have I learned after taking this journey and reliving every dumb ass decision about men I've ever made? Well, I've learned that I am a die-hard romantic; I am too forgiving and a little bit naive. Just a little you're thinking? Okay, very naive. But on a deeper level; I need to feel needed, I need to feel loved and I need to feel like I belong to someone. There, I said it. Though I am a mother, sister, daughter, grand-daughter, aunt, friend, boss and much more; I need a man to validate me. I have just saved thousands of dollars on therapy. Now, the dilemma is how to fix me. Okay, that may have to be addressed in book 2 but like a true addict, admitting that there is a problem is half the battle. I have also learned that you can't change people, especially at this age. Maybe a young twenty-something year old can be molded and trained but at thirty-something, it is what it is. People can't be how you want them to be. If he's moody, he's moody. If he's cheap, he's cheap. There's nothing you can say, do or suggest that's going to change that and even if there was, why would you want to because then they're just doing it because you want them to. I want a man or a friend even to be how they are because that's how they are. Not because I asked them to be that way. For me, this lesson is paramount. You be you, I be me and if that's works then it's beautiful.

Another important lesson I've learned is that I need to learn to love me. Until I do, I will not be able to make anyone happy nor will they be able to make me happy. I have to be happy with myself and looking back at these pages; I have a long way to go. I am not proud of some of the decisions I've made or the relationships that I let continue when it was clear that it was time for them to end. I ignored the signs and these were not subtle signs, they were in-your-face, wake-the-fuck-up signs. I compromised myself time and time again and for what? I'm not saying that I was totally without fault or the perfect partner as I clearly did wrong as well but we all need to know when it's right. And if it aint right, let it go. Let it go before someone gets hurt. Know when to walk away and be woman or man enough to do so.

My focus in life is not to find a partner-in-crime or a Clyde to my Bonnie but to enjoy what is meant to be the best decade of my life. 40 is the new 20 they say and I'm so ready to live life without the drama or the heartache. It's all about enjoying the things that make me truly happy; my children, my family, my friends and my career. And if Mr. Right happens to come along in the midst of all that then fine otherwise, I'll be okay.

Ex update:

- Baby Daddy spent the next 17 or so years in Georgia with the same woman he cheated on me with. Funniest thing, she and I actually ended up being very cool with each other. Whenever I sent my son to visit them, she always made sure he was well taken care of. She was the one who called on Christmases and birthdays. They had 3 children together and he had 1 outside (meaning one with a different woman while he was still with her). Eventually she wised up and kicked his sorry ass out. Last I heard he was living somewhere in Staten Island with yet another woman but he and my son have still not really connected.
- Shorty continued on a downward spiral, never quite getting back on his feet. I heard he started hanging out a lot, smoking weed and never really holding down a proper job. My brother says he also lost about 5 teeth. Over the years, I have seen him from time to time. We are cordial but never anything more.
- Dexter married the same girlfriend that he had way back then. They have 3 children and are holding on. We speak occasionally and see each other in social situations a few times a year. And he is still begging for us to have sex just one more time. No.
- James and I are still good friends, well the kind of friends that can call on each other when there's a problem. We keep in touch via Facebook or text and see each other from time to time socially. He's happily married with three children and way more than a pot to piss in and plenty windows

to throw it out of. He had moved from Trinidad to Canada then finally settled right here in Brooklyn, New York.

- Frank, ah yes Frank. Well he turned out to a pathological liar though I never quite found out the true story. It seems no one knew exactly what it was. I bumped into him a few years later in Trinidad; he apparently fled there after getting himself into some sort of trouble. A few months later, they caught up to him; he was shot and killed.
- Scruffy lives between Trinidad and Tobago; he will never be able to return to America. My daughter visits him once or twice a year and he's as good a dad as one can be living over 2,000 miles from their child. He never remarried nor had any more children. I often wonder if we would still be together if he had never gotten deported.
- The Wuss is in a long-term relationship; they have a daughter together. We have seen each other a couple of times over the years and when I see him, it tugs at my heart for a brief moment, very brief thankfully. He has asked about me a few times through my sister-in-law, complaining about how unhappy he is in his present situation. Oh well.
- The Jamaican had a son the year after we broke up but we remained cool with each other up until Bubba got involved. He continued to pay just minimum payments on my credit card bill despite me asking him numerous times to double up or transfer the balance onto his own or his girlfriend's card. I heard excuse after excuse. I eventually told him, as directed by Bubba, who owned a credit repair company, that I would have to hand the

collections over to a company unless he could double up. Bubba called him pretending to be that company then the Jamaican texted me, cursed me out and refused to pay any more; in fact, he said the car was a gift from me to him for all that he did for me while we were together. Since I didn't have any proof of our arrangement; I got stuck with the bill. Ladies, lesson learned. Do not sign anything for anyone without a notarized contract!

- I haven't laid eyes on Bubbalicious since he came by to collect his things and not pay me back. I have heard through reliable sources that he is well. I hope our paths continue not to cross.
- Daddy of the Year—we could write a whole book just about this one. At the time this book went to publish, he has never admitted to lying nor do I ever expect him to. Even if he's not lying, he still isn't trying very hard to convince me otherwise. I won't lie and say that I don't still think about him but I will say that I hope to never go down that path again. We still talk, we still text each other and see each other occasionally but at the end of the day, I have to love *me* more than any love I give to another. And that's something I'm still working on.

The End